CLARITY IS POWER

Q & A

"Clarity is Power" book series, is a collection of wisdom from thought-provoking Q and A with renowned Mahatria. His unique gift of answering questions spontaneously is captured in this book, offering life-changing insights.

The "Clarity is Power" series comprises 11 illuminating volumes, each addressing essential aspects of life:

1. Attitudes
2. Self-Discipline
3. Emotional Development
4. Relationships
5. Marriage
6. Parenting
7. Student Life
8. Career Growth
9. Leadership and Entrepreneurship
10. Spirituality
11. Faith

Mahatria Spiritualist | Thought leader | Diviner of infinitheism

For nearly three decades, Mahatria has empowered millions worldwide to achieve holistic abundance. His profound wisdom uplifts people in health, wealth, love, bliss, and spirituality.

infinitheism, the path divined by Mahatria, inspires breakthroughs for anyone who ardently desires abundance by transforming the human spirit to have faith in its infinite potential.

First published in India

MANJUL

Manjul Publishing House

• 2nd Floor, Usha Preet Complex,
42 Malviya Nagar, Bhopal 462 003 - India
• C-16, Sector 3, Noida, Uttar Pradesh 201301 – India
Website: www.manjulindia.com

Distribution Centres:
Ahmedabad, Bengaluru, Bhopal, Kolkata, Chennai,
Hyderabad, Mumbai, New Delhi, Pune

In association with:

infinitheism

3, 3rd Cross Road, R A Puram,
Chennai, Tamil Nadu, India
www.infinitheism.com

PARENTING (CLARITY IS POWER)

by

mahatria Ra

This edition first published in 2016
Third impression 2024

ISBN 978-93-5543-435-7

Printed and bound in India by Thomson Press (India) Ltd.

CLARITY IS POWER

Q&A

PARENTING

mahātria

CONTENTS

CONTENTS

1

In spite of adopting the best practices, I find handling my 13-year-old child very difficult. Please help.

Parenting should always happen with this faith in the background that 'Irrespective of how they are and what they are today, my children will do very well in life one day'. The thoughts of parents are constant vibrations that children inherit and there is a spiritual significance to the whole thing. Your most dominant thoughts of your children will have the greatest bearing on what your children will become in life. So think right, think positive, and think of a bright future irrespective of their present.

Two, correct your vocabulary. We don't handle children - we handle machines. We relate to children. There is a respect that a 13-year-old deserves and expects. Give that respect to the 13-year-old. For many of us, our expressions of love lack that respect, and love is not love if there is no respect in the expressions of love.

When the fruit ripens and drops by itself, it is the process of growing. It is another thing altogether when you pluck the fruit from the tree. Haven't you seen that the tree then bleeds milk? Similarly, the disobedience of a 13-year-old is one of the expressions of growing years. Every facet of life has its own expressions. When we forcefully truncate the expressions of these growing years, the implications of these will come out in ugly ways in the later years.

Premature disciplining of a child finds expression in a very adamant childhood. Premature truncation of childhood finds expression in a very indifferent adolescence. Premature truncation of adolescence finds expression in apathetic adulthood. Premature truncation of adulthood results in an attention seeking, nagging, complaining, interfering and lecturing old age.

So what to do? First, believe that your child will do very well in life and keep sending out these vibrations. Canalize their energy into developing talents. Enrol them in post school classes to develop their talent, which will also open them up to a newer circle of friends. Most importantly, love them with respect even if they are not showing that respect to you as yet. It will eventually rub off on them.

“

The thoughts of parents are constant vibrations that children inherit and there is a spiritual significance to the whole thing.

mahātria

2

My son is 15 years old. In spite of constantly telling him to be polite and not to get angry, he is very short-tempered. He gets angry even at small things. I find it very difficult to handle him.

Talking about someone's weakness won't help them overcome that weakness. The more you keep focusing on weaknesses - both yours as well as others, the more you will fuel their growth.

You can't give up something, but you can always embrace something. When you embrace strength, you weaken the weakness. When one's attachment for the lower grows into an attachment for the higher, the lower falls on its own accord. We don't give up in life, but we go up.

Humans are designed to step out of the lower rungs of the ladder because of their inclination to step onto the higher rungs. They are not giving up the lower rungs. They are, as a matter of fact, going up the higher rungs.

All of us need a relationship in which we won't be held against ourselves. I have my strengths and I also have my weaknesses. I do have my shortcomings. What I need is, a relationship in which my lesser side is not constantly provoked and instigated. I want someone who will always relate to my better side. I want that one relationship in which my positive qualities will always be brought to the surface, the presence of which will make my negative qualities fade away in the course of time.

Good parenting is not about nagging the children by rubbing them on the wrong side, but about showing them their right side and grooming their right side. Your child must be surrounded by a world that consistently brings their lesser side onto the surface.

Take this parental challenge and consistently bring the higher and positive side of the child onto the surface and in due course, anger will drop by itself. ●

“

You can't give up something,
but you can always
embrace something.

When you embrace strength,
you weaken the weakness.

When one's attachment
for the lower
grows into an attachment
for the higher,
the lower falls on its own accord.

We don't give up in life,
but we go up.

mahātria

We will have our first baby in less than a month from now. Seeking your guidance as to what should we do and not do, to grow into the best parents our baby can have.

Every time I see a new born, the first question has always been, "Whom does the child resemble?" My reply always is, "The child looks like herself. He looks like himself." The greatest wonder of life isn't the similarities that each new born brings into this world, but the uniqueness it brings along with its birth. What it means is to realise that in the history of the world, there has been nobody like the one that has come, and there will be no one like this one. In His creation, there are no repetitions. With the birth of every child and its first crying, the world hears a voice never heard before - never in the history of the universe.

So, the first parental responsibility is to celebrate the uniqueness of the child. Never compare your child with any other for any reason. Comparison reveals differences and differences will lead to feeling superior or inferior - neither of which is good.

Babies need attention. The more attention they get, the more demonstrative they will grow. The crying of the child always gains attention. Somehow the child is not given enough attention during its happy moments. A behaviour recognised and rewarded will be repeated - positive or negative. Too much attention to crying and not much attention to its happiness will send wrong signals. So, ensure that there is a lot of recognition and acknowledgement for the child during their best moods.

Don't hide the child from visitors. Sometimes our love can be so protective that we do not expose the little ones to various kinds of people. Exposure to multiple hands will aid the child in growing without inhibitions. Even if it appears that they do not understand, keep talking to the child and keep reading to the child. It tremendously aids brain development.

Environment is one of the strongest factors in the development of a child. Will they hear lots and lots of laughter in their growing years or will it be shouting and snarling, which will be their environment? Will they be conditioned by television noises or will they grow listening to lots and lots of human communication within the family? Let the child arrive in an environment of expressive love, demonstrative happiness and bonds of communication. ●

“

A behaviour recognised and rewarded will be repeated - positive or negative.

mahātria

4

How do we explain to the adolescent children that a wrong does not become right just because everybody does it?

This is the story of most teenagers...

Their friends should accept them otherwise they feel left out. If a few of their classmates smoke, they too are tempted to take a puff. If a few in their peer group cut classes, then they too want to join the bandwagon. If a few watch unethical sites, they too would desire that. If some friends nickname a teacher, the rest in the class also join in.

Peer acceptance - that's all that matters during adolescence. They crave to be part of a friend's gang. Without that gang they feel incomplete.

Let us understand, why they want to belong to a peer group?

In a peer group there is collective ego, and the collective ego is a complete ego whereas individual ego is an incomplete ego. To feel the completeness in the collective ego, they crave to belong to a group.

To be accepted in a peer group, they end up doing whatever others do. Otherwise, they feel they will be left out. If they are left out, they will feel very lonely and during adolescence loneliness could be disastrous.

What can we do as parents?

1. Help them to build a healthy self-image, so that they feel complete unto themselves.

With their self-image intact, they will not crave for peer acceptance. Of course, they will enjoy it if it is there, but not stoop down to do wrong activities, just to earn an endorsement from their friends. In a situation, even if peer acceptance is not there, they will be able to deal with it on the strength of the healthy self-image they have about themselves. What others think of them will not make a difference anymore.

How to build a healthy self-image in our children?

Appreciate them lavishly whenever they do the right things. The issue with us is, we mostly do third-party appreciation. We talk about how proud we are about them to our friends and relatives, not to them directly. They never get to know that you as a parent value them and their thoughts a lot. Do not be shy of direct appreciation. Catch them when they are right and appreciate them.

If 8 times children are appreciated for whatever is right and good about them and 2 times you tell them subtly where they need to correct themselves, they will listen to you. That would be the right balance. Not the vice versa.

2. Talk to them about things that they are interested in.

   Children consider you interesting only if you talk to them about what they are interested in. For example, if I can talk about European Premium League and La Liga with my children regularly, one day they wouldn't mind listening to me about Bhagavad Gita. If you do not know about their interests, ask them to explain so that you can understand. It is a nice place to begin the conversation. Become their friend; approach them as a friend...

3. Remember, the need to feel respected outweighs the need for growth; the need to be appreciated takes precedence over the need for advice; the need to be 'what I want to be' is a primary need, while the need to be 'what you want me to be' is only a secondary need.

   At every stage, we are standing on one pedestal of life and judging those on the other pedestals, and this has led to disharmony in relationships at a personal level and a disharmonious world at a global level. At every age, we seem to suffer from amnesia about the phases we have passed through... Don't be too quick in judging them. Let us attempt to understand the fragility of adolescence and help them to become strong mentally and emotionally.

Parenting is an art especially in today's context. Let's learn to be a skilful artist here!

Remember,
the need to feel respected
outweighs the need for growth;
the need to be appreciated
takes precedence
over the need for advice.

mahātria

If I praise my children, they become overconfident and that causes them to fail. If I criticise them, they get disheartened and that causes them to fail. So, what should be my approach?

The complexity of individuals is that they need an image, as well as, a reflection. What a person feels about themselves and the image they hold of themselves is one of the biggest factors in their performance. But at the same time, if shortfalls, inadequacies, compromises, mistakes, and errors are not reflected back to them, they will remain mediocre, assuming their standards are good enough. Below par performances need feedback. Without constructive criticism the bar of performance will never be raised. Ideally, you need to criticise the performance and encourage the performer.

That's why it's essential to encourage individuals, lift their image, and enhance their performing abilities. And yet, offer feedback, provide constructive criticism, and reflect on the gap between what can be and what is.

So, discuss the mistakes but don't make the individual feel as if they are the wrong person. Help them understand that failure is an event, and it is not a reflection of their entire self. Teach them to deal with the failure but don't make them feel like a failure. Just because they have failed in a few things, it doesn't mean they won't succeed in any.

Leaders, parents, and teachers succeed only when they help individuals enjoy a healthy image of themselves, and at the same time also reflect their shortcomings to them. Individuals have to be helped to feel good even if what they have done is not good enough. And at the same time, since everything can be improved, even a good enough performance must be encouraged to be bettered. Performances are about the individual, but they do not define the individual. Disassociate the performance from the performer while giving feedback on the performance. Separate the person from their actions. Criticize the actions but praise the individual.

Let the painter know that you respect their abilities. But let them also know that this piece of a painting could be better. Let your child know that they have infinite potential. But let them also know, with such potential, their performances must be a lot better. Never miss a single opportunity to encourage an individual. Never miss a chance to offer honest criticism of the performance.

I once had a boss who always told me, "Hey, you are so good that no target is big enough for you." Thus, he made me feel capable. However, when I achieved my targets, he always commented, "If a target is achieved, then the target was wrong." Thus, he raised the bar for my performance. He not only helped me to rise in my own eyes - he taught me to look up to myself, but also helped me to always raise the bar of my performance - he taught me that I should consistently outperform my own standards.

I want my son to be an all rounder in life. So I have enrolled him in many classes after school hours. Sometimes I feel that I am unreasonable in pushing him. What should I do?

The son is not interested in having a formal training in music. However, the father and grandfather have been traditionally rooted in classical music. So the boy is forced to learn music. Unless the heart is rooted, talents don't branch out. The boy prefers his basketball coaching to music classes.

Excellence isn't something that can be thrust upon. The urge for excellence has to come from within. The boy doesn't do well in singing. His music teachers criticise him, "Coming from such an illustrious family it is a shame that you don't have a grasp for music." The family condemns him saying, "Don't spoil the family name. Basketball will not feed you. Dump it and focus on music." Everybody screams, "Practice more." How much ever you may practice, a donkey's bray will never become a horse's neigh. In not being able to live up to the expectations of his loved ones the boy feels less about himself. This feeling, "May be, I am not good enough," begins to show up in his academic performances too.

It is prime parental responsibility to give children avenues by which they feel like a success and not to thrust upon them the paths in which they feel like a failure. From relationships to careers, exercise to spirituality, more than 'what I do', 'how I feel about it' forms the foundation for the future.

The issue isn't basketball or music. During growing years, either in academics or in sports or in theatre or in arts or in social work, etc., the path is immaterial, but in some path children should feel a taste of success. A girl who feels that sense of success in BA Economics will do much better with her future than the girl who feels like a failure in BE Electronics.

Success or failure is not about potential, but it is a matter of interest. The mind will easily follow the heart, but the heart seldom follows the mind. Competence cannot cause passion, but passion can always develop competence.

Give your child a chance by choosing a path where his best will come out. Not everybody can be good at everything, but everybody can be good at something. Finding that for our children is our greatest parental responsibility.

Excellence isn't something that can be thrust upon. The urge for excellence has to come from within.

mahātria

7

How can I improve my relationship with my child?

The quality of your communication with your child determines the quality of your relationships with them. Communication is everything in parenting.

The key is to take the child's perspective into consideration and then communicate. Unless you see the world the way they see it, you will not be able to transform them, to see the world the way you see it. Good parenting is in the ability to step into the child's shoes and then helping them to walk in the direction that is good for them. A good mother cannot parent all her children with the same methodology. There is no one way for all. Leadership and parenting has to be customised.

It isn't just how you cook; how you serve also makes a difference. Communication achieves its objective only when all the three components are taken care of. They are - 'What you say?', 'How you say it?' and 'When you say it'. Communicate only to a prepared mind.

Good communication will serve a relationship. ●

8

My 9-year-old child keeps comparing himself with others and feels he is good for nothing. Please help me to deal with his behaviour.

Self-belief is not built by giving speeches to a child. It is built by giving the child victorious experiences. With every taste of victory the child grows in his own eyes.

We cannot hide from the fact that as humans we have our prejudices. At home, at school, and in the society, unintentionally we extend more attention to a few and less to the rest. Thinking we are challenging them for their own good, we tend to benchmark the rest with the few. And, when this happens with children, it does dent their self-image.

Even if you decide to correct your parenting in this aspect, still your child will be exposed to the larger world. So let the world be what it is... Let us work on the child.

Children need small victories for them to start believing in themselves. One of the prime responsibilities in parenting is to create the context in which children taste these small victories.

Confidence grows only when you do things that you have never done before, or do things that you think you cannot. So, it is important to provide children with horizontal exposure of getting them to do very many things for the first time. And, it is equally important that they taste victorious results in some of these processes. Somehow, as parents and teachers, we are so focussed on their improvement that we fail to realise children are not going to gain confidence out of never-ending processes.

Net practice after net practice is not going to make him feel like a cricketer; just one real match experience and a little performance in that match will truly make him feel like a cricketer. Singing classes after singing classes... the mere process of development is not enough for a 9-year-old. Just get him to sing amongst relatives and a few words of appreciation and encouragement will make a humongous difference.

For children to sustain a process they have to taste results. With results comes self-belief. Self-belief will induce further involvement in the process, which will result in consistent results and thus a greater self-belief. That's the cycle... Because the child is just a 9-year-old, the responsibility to keep the cycle going is a parental responsibility.

Think positively, do not get desperate when things don't happen at the pace at which you want, remember your child is only 9, have this faith that you can turn them around, keep communicating long enough, and fill their life with small victories. Children are God's very own, placed in your parental care. You can make all the difference. ●

For children to sustain a process they have to taste results.

With results comes self-belief.

Self-belief will induce further involvement in the process, which will result in consistent results and thus a greater self-belief.

That's the cycle...

mahātria

How to deal with the emotional tantrums and bad behaviour of my children?

Children exhibit bad behaviour because he/she is not getting enough attention. We take a well-behaved child for granted, don't we? It's not that your son cannot study by himself; it's just that he enjoys the attention he gets when you sit along with him to study. It's not that your daughter wants to throw temper tantrums; she helplessly resorts to all the bad when she doesn't get enough attention for all the good in her. It's not that the adolescent at home wants to speak on the phone for 45 minutes; what we need to understand here is that for those 45 minutes, someone at the other end of the phone is making your son/daughter feel like a king/queen. Children drift away from parental control when someone in the world makes them feel more wanted than the parents.

During growing years, children are obviously not self-sufficient with their self-image. They are dependent on the world around them. Awards, rewards, demonstrative appreciation, and expressive validations give them a sense of fulfilment because they confirm that children have drawn enough attention from parents and teachers. The more attention they receive, the more they feel wanted. 'Attention seeking' is one of the basic needs of every being.

A globally renowned spiritualist leader once remarked, "Good or bad, I don't care; but I want the media to keep writing about me." If not the right way, at least the wrong way, people need attention. In America, a man randomly shot at people on the street, wounding many and killing a few. He later said, "I didn't know how else to make the headlines in the newspaper." When we don't know the right way to gain attention, we resort to any available way to gain it. Tantrums and bad behaviour is drawing attention the wrong way.

The point is that there is a tender heart within each child that needs attention. If the child is not given attention, they resort to bad behaviour to draw that attention. A hungry man needs food, not criticism. Seeking attention is a sort of psychological hunger. This isn't something to complain about. This is, but, human frailty. This is something that needs compassion and understanding. After all, we too go through this predicament.

Any behavioural change can be achieved by giving attention to the positive behaviours you want and more importantly, by ignoring the negative behaviours you don't want. Feed attention to the behaviours you want more from children. Starve attention to those behaviours you want them to stop. Catch children when they are right, recognise and reward them for that, and soon the behaviour will change. ●

A hungry man needs food,
not criticism.
Seeking attention is a sort of
psychological hunger.

This isn't something to complain about.
This is, but, human frailty.

This is something that needs
compassion and understanding.

mahātria

With the arrival of
my second child,
my first child has
become very adamant.
This is despite giving
enough attention
to my first child.
What should I do?

Human beings by nature are attention seekers. And there is nothing called 'enough attention' in the realm of relationships.

You feel you are giving 'enough attention'; but the recipient is not feeling so. When more is given, more will be expected, and you have to service this attention.

Every parent must understand that a child did not ask to be born. It is you, who decided to bring the child into existence. It's a responsibility that you had decided to shoulder and now you have to execute this responsibility.

Your first child is not bothered, whether he is getting enough attention or not. His point is his mother's attention is now being divided between him and his sibling. And nobody likes divided attention.

His adamancy is just a way, an expression by which he is asking you for some exclusive, undivided attention and time. Explore activities which you can do exclusively only with your first child. Only 'you and him' walk or a movie or simply a visit to the nearby ice-cream shop should do the trick for you. Go creative!

Importantly when you are with him, talk to him about his interests, what he likes and dislikes and never talk about the second born. Keep on investing exclusive time and you will see that your first born will settle down.

Your husband must be feeling the same, ever since the children have come, he is no more getting the sort of attention he used to get from you!

So, anytime the world is crying for attention, they're just saying that they are not getting enough undivided attention from you. Find a way to create those time compartments to give them undivided attention. You will see a phenomenal change.

“

Your first child is not bothered, whether he is getting enough attention or not. His point is his mother's attention is now being divided between him and his sibling. And nobody likes divided attention.

mahātria

What is my role in making my child a legend?

The world-class citizens of tomorrow are developed in the cocoon of homes today by the responsible hands of parents. The seed must be taught when it is still a seed on how to be a tree.

At a time when there is exaggerated focus on which school, which college, and which institution a child should pursue education, are we grossly underestimating the role of parenting in the making of an individual? Has there ever been a greater institution than parents and family? Institutions build professionals. Parents develop the person. Much more than the time children have at school, the time they have with parents is going to have a greater bearing on their character. I am not undermining the role of educational institutions, but I am emphasising the role of parenting, and without an iota of doubt parents are the primary architects in the development of character in children.

How often we hear Sachin Tendulkar say, "My father always told me..." and "My brother used to tell me..." When Yuvraj Singh was asked about his comeback, his reply began, "My mother is a very strong lady..."

It was Jawaharlal Nehru who told his daughter Indira Gandhi, "You will often find your life splitting into two roads - one, the easy and the crowded and the other, the tough and less crowded. Take the less crowded and that will make all the difference." Much later in her life, Indira Gandhi acknowledged, "That is exactly what I did and that has made all the difference." Mahatma Gandhi's mother told him: "Even while in London, you will not touch meat, women and alcohol." Much later in his life, Gandhiji acknowledged, "I exactly did that and those years shaped the character of my life."

In fact, any time you admire somebody for their character and ask them to speak about it, almost every time, they will begin, "My grandfather used to tell me" or "I have always seen my grandmother doing this" or "My father told me once" or "This I learnt from my mother." The reason is very obvious. We learn much more by what we see than what we hear.

That's why the primary responsibility in parenting is to be a role model worth emulating. The only scripture most children read is the life of their parents because they get to watch it from the closest proximity. The life of parents is the only Quran they will read in their lifetime; the only Vedas they will see; the only Bible they will experience; the only Dhammapada they will imbibe; and the only Dharma they will follow. As parents, your life will either serve as a warning or an example to your children. I know it is an awesome responsibility, but how else can you explain why you came into this planet before them and then took the initiative to bring them to this planet.

Every child is a rare, unique, original, masterpiece... Master's piece. Don't mould them into a showpiece.

He is here to be 'he', she is here to be 'she' and no one else. So, preserve the originality of the child. Communicate enough to your child and instil in them the confidence that just because a group of their friends do not accept them as they are, there is no necessity for them to drop their originality. The more and more parents appreciate children for what they are, children will never have to stoop down in order to gain recognition. It is only when children are starved from appreciation at home, they lose themselves to gain someone else. When parents take the responsibility to preserve and build the self-image of the child, they will understand that the group that doesn't accept them is not their world. It is easy to be one in the crowd. It needs courage to be different from the crowd. And what your child will be, will depend on the role you play as parents in shaping his/her self-image.

How much ever scientifically explained, parenting is still an art that parents have to customise according to the temperament of their children. Children, basically God's creation, have been entrusted in the hands of parents in the trust that you will play your part. Please play your part diligently. It is worth everything when you realise you have an opportunity to parent a world-class citizen.

People ask me often, what is the purpose of life? Apart from all that you may discover, parenting is certainly one of the purposes... Serve the purpose. ●

I am a teacher and a mom.
I invest a lot of time
with my teenage daughter
to make her study well.
But 'You don't love me'
is what I hear from her
these days. In spite of
doing everything,
to hear this
is very painful.
Please help me.

Every role has some inherent primary responsibilities. No matter what else you do, if you falter in your primary responsibilities of that role, then eventually the relationship will fall apart.

I know how it feels after doing so much for your adolescent daughter and then to get to hear from her, "You don't love me." As a parent you are so focused on their development and you do your best for her - best schools, best coaching classes, private study rooms, and what not.

But if you are not there to respect her emotions, if you don't have the time to have conversations with her, if your lap isn't available when she is low, if your hands don't reach out when her tears trickle down, if you don't give her the feeling that she is more important to you than her performances... then you have failed in your primary responsibilities as a parent.

You have donned the role of a teacher and a coach, but where is the parent? On the contrary, no matter how affectionate a teacher or a coach may be, if they do not focus on the development and performance of the child, then they fail in the primary responsibilities of their chosen role.

The success of a role does not depend on what all you do. It only depends on how well you execute the primary responsibilities of the role. Don't cry 'foul', when people blame you for not doing justice to the relationship. Stop quoting all that you have done for the relationship. Shut Up! Instead, simply introspect, "Am I doing justice to the primary responsibilities of the role?"

Teaching can be delegated to a coaching center. Your primary responsibility is to be a parent. She will make you a proud parent. ●

“

Every role has some inherent primary responsibilities. No matter what else you do, if you falter in your primary responsibilities of that role, then eventually the relationship will fall apart.

mahātria

13

Should parents expect their child to serve them?

You get attached to what you serve. You get attached to whom you serve. Seems strange! In receiving so much, the receiver should feel the attachment for the giver; but, in reality, the giver feels more attached to the receiver than the other way around.

That's why, traditionally, even in the supposedly a 'receiving' relationship, like God, Guru, and society, you were asked to serve them. Though the truth is, the benefit of the vibrations a devotee receives from a place of worship are much more than anything they can give to the place of worship, they were asked to serve the place of worship. It is in serving the place one will feel the attachment to the place, and it is in feeling the attachment to the place they will feel one with the place, and it is only in feeling one with the place, they can inherit the vibrations of that place.

Though the seeker will receive infinitely more than what they can ever give to a Guru, the seeker is asked to serve the Guru in all possible ways. More than just being with the Guru, representing the cause of the Guru is considered a greater blessing. But, why? Who needs whom?

It is in serving the Guru they will feel the attachment to the Guru, and it is in feeling the attachment to the Guru they will connect with the Guru, and in connecting with the Guru they will dissolve into the Guru, and in dissolving into the Guru they will find the path and purpose of their life.

In serving the society, you actually serve yourself. You don't liberate the other through your service. You serve for your salvation. Speaking about those who give, Khalil Gibran said, "Through the hands of such as these God speaks, and from behind their eyes He smiles upon the Earth."

It is by giving, we truly receive. It is in serving, we are truly served. It is in losing ourselves to something, we gain everything.

More than you choosing a *Seva* (selfless service), blessed are those, whom a *Seva* chooses. Read the term *Seva* as something you do with your personal involvement and not just writing a cheque of donation.

So, as parents, apart from everything you do for your children - young and grown up, create the contexts for them to serve you. The theory of you wanting to be independent and not dependent on anybody is good for you, but not good for your children. It is in serving you, they will learn to value elders.

As educators, apart from the education you choose to impart to your students, create the contexts for them to serve you, as well as, the school. A sense of belonging can never be created in the students unless they get to do something for the school and the teachers.

As heads of organisations, let the employees get involved in celebrating certain occasions in the organisational premises.

Teaching a child not to step on the grasshopper is as important to the child as to the grasshopper.

Learning to serve is more important to you than what you serve. There is only one way to feel ONE with anything - SERVE.

My teenage daughter spends a lot of time dressing up. It becomes a bone of contention between us. Should I just allow her to be herself?

Your teenage daughter is going through enormous changes both physically and emotionally. She wants to perpetually stand in front of the mirror, and see the changes in her body from all angles. She is concerned about her looks. She wants to speak about her emotions. She is experiencing new cravings and wants to talk about it. She is using new accessories that she is curious about.

These are expressions of her growing years. If these expressions are not recognised at home, then she will befriend someone from the outside world and may even get exploited by that someone who is able to empathise with the expressions of her growing years.

Parents fight with their children insisting that they should only wear the clothes which they think are right for their children. Parents take children for shopping and override the choices of their children in terms of what they think is right - not just the type of clothes but even the colours. From the hair band to the earring to the belt to the footwear... everything is interfered with.

Why can't we allow our children to choose what they want to wear? Neither does modern wear make a person vulgar nor does traditional attire guarantee a pious person... Dressing is again an expression of growing years... nothing more than that.

It is one thing when the fruit ripens and drops itself off. That is outgrowing. It had lived its lifespan as a vegetable, outgrown into a fruit, ripened into its old age and then fallen off. This is the natural process of growing and outgrowing. It is totally another thing when you pluck the fruit from the tree. Haven't you seen that the tree then bleeds milk? This bleeding is not just the bleeding of the tree but the bleeding of life expressed through the tree.

Every facet has its own lifespan and any premature truncation of that phase causes this bleeding. Aren't we familiar with the terms premature delivery and premature death? This isn't just related to the birth of a child or the death of a person who died when still young...

Any forced truncation of 'hood' infanthood, childhood, boyhood/girlhood, manhood... is both the premature death of the earlier 'hood' and the premature delivery of the next 'hood' and it causes bleeding of some form.

Any premature truncation of 'hood' continues to crave from within and they find expression in a later phase of life. Premature weaning from breast feeding finds expression in the child sucking his thumb... Premature disciplining of a child finds expression in a very adamant boyhood... Premature truncation of the boyhood finds expression in a very indifferent adolescence... Premature truncation of adolescence finds expression in a very apathetic adulthood...

Allow the bud to bloom into a flower through the natural process... and the flower looks so beautiful. Instead, forcefully open the petals of the bud and create a forced flowering... see, how ugly the flower looks... not only does it look ugly, even that poetic fragrance of the flower will be missing.

The expression of every 'hood' during the 'hood' is so beautiful, natural and lively. Seed to the plant, plant to the tree, tree into flowering, flowering into a vegetable, vegetable into a fruit, from the fruit again the seeds... this is life. Any intrusion turns it ugly. ●

My 2-year-old child has become very adamant now. She cries for everything and has become very demanding. Few months back she was not like this. I do not know how to deal with this?

Actually, what is happening is that, your 2-year-old child is able to understand a lot of what others are speaking and wants to reciprocate. But she is unable to express because she hasn't developed the vocabulary needed to express all that she wants to express. She finds herself wanting when it comes to expressing herself. She is frustrated with herself for this inadequacy and angry at others' inability to grasp her clues. She is yearning with infinite expressions but finds herself so helpless with just a few words and gestures, that sometimes they get expressed with a smile and other times through crying.

Of course, you can be a tough parent, regiment the child with admonishments - both physical and verbal and can even take control over the child. The child may even sober down... but you will then have to face the carry-over of this crankiness in the youth of that child, and be sure, you will find it even more difficult to handle it at that phase of life.

The next time you hear a crying, be compassionate. Somebody needs your attention. The next time you witness an emotional drama, be compassionate. Somebody needs your attention. One of the deepest of human cravings is the need to be heard and the need to be attended to. The solution is simple: Take the initiative to give her enough attention, preferably, to her positive qualities. Be demonstrative. Be vocal. Develop expressiveness. Invest quality time.

The crankiness you see in your child is a part of her growing years. She will soon outgrow this too. ●